Y0-EGG-897

WorkBook

My Community

HELPERS AND PLACES

DreamTivity

Community

Do you live in a **Community**? Sure you do! A community includes all the people and places near your home and neighborhood, and in your town or city. You may live in a large community with many houses, stores, offices, and workers. Or your community may be smaller, with farmhouses and a town center.

A community provides needed services and goods, such as medical care, education, groceries, recreation, and firefighters. By working together, all the busy people in a community contribute to everyone's well-being.

The most important members of your community are your family. Draw the people in your family—and include your pets! Do you have close relatives that live nearby? Include them, too!

People in communities live in **houses**, **apartments**, **mobile homes**, and **condos**. (Some harbor towns have **houseboats**!) No matter where you live, this is home. Home is your comfy place.

Draw your home—either the outside, or your favorite room in your home.

What's so special about your place, anyway?

Built for Community

All across your community there are buildings used for different services.

Where do you go when you are sick? _____

Where do you go when your pet is sick? _____

Which is a house of worship? _____

Where do you see a judge? _____

Where is the mayor? _____

Where does your car get fixed? _____

Courthouse

Church

Mechanic's Garage

Hospital

City Hall

Veterinarian

Community Helpers have special jobs or responsibilities. Some are **emergency services**, others **essential services** (that we all need), and others are **regular services**. Draw lines to match each to the job.

police officer

pilot

chef

nurse

mechanic

hairdresser

firefighter

politician

farmer

teacher

Down at the Park

Do you have a community **Park**? It may have a playground,
basketball courts, benches, a pond, or open space to run.
It's time to play at the park! Can you find... four balls?
An owl? A worm? Some bugs? Something... impossible?
How many can you find: bikes, birds, dogs, and toys?
What's for lunch? Who's ahead—3 or 5?

Police

Do you have a **Police Station** in your community? This is where **Police Officers** report for work and where police cars are kept. Police officers are always ready to come to the scene of an accident or crime. They are important members of the community who help keep us safe.

A police officer may come to your school to teach kids about the laws of the community that they must follow. Laws aren't just for grownups! Laws help the people in a community stay safe and get along with each other.

Do you ride a bike or skateboard? The law says: wear a safety helmet! Do you ever need to cross a busy street? The law says: only cross at a crosswalk! Do you ever wonder what's on the other side of someone's fence? The law says: do not trespass! Do you ever play outside and lose track of time? The law says: always be home in time for dinner! (Oh, wait.... that's a family rule, not a law.)

Which officer arrives at the accident?

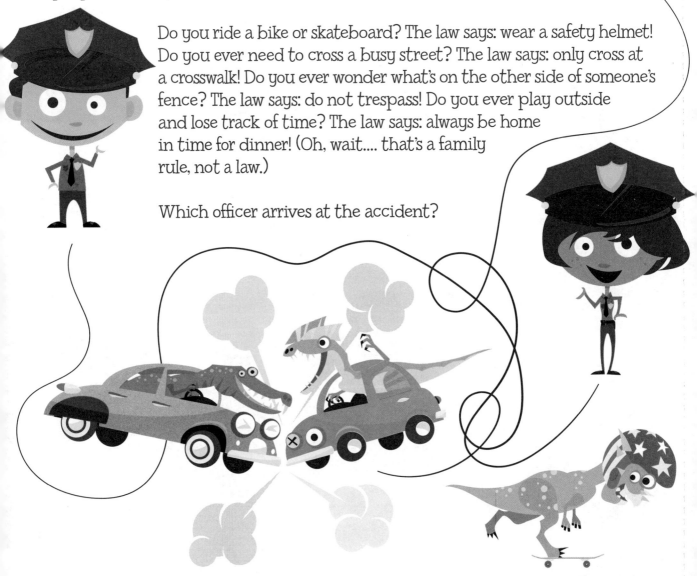

Have you ever been stuck in a traffic jam in your community?
Too many cars. Some days going places takes longer than others.

Only 4 vehicles are identical in all four quadrants. Find them.

Fire Station

Do you have a **Fire Station** in your community? This is where fire trucks are kept. **Firefighters** are ready at all times to zoom to the rescue when there is fire or smoke reported.

Firefighters hook a large hose up to a fire hydrant to tap into the water supply. It's like a big faucet! Firefighters use long ladders to reach the top levels of a building.

Firefighters may come to your school to teach about **Fire Safety**.

Always keep a bucket of water ready at a campfire! Never play with matches, lighters, or lit candles!

If a fire breaks out in your home or a building:

SHOUT and GET OUT!
Yell out **FIRE**! and keep yelling as you quickly get out of the building to your **safe meeting place**. Once outside, find a grownup to call **911** for help!

STAY LOW and GO!
If you are in a building and you smell smoke, fall and crawl! **Smoke rises** in the room, so **stay low** to the ground and go to the nearest door or window. If the door is hot, go another way.

STOP! DROP! And ROLL!
If your hair or clothes catch fire—**DON'T RUN**! **Stop where you are**, **drop to the ground**, **cover your face** and **roll around** to put out the flame. If possible, have someone wet you down with cool water.

Safe Meeting Place
Talk with your parents so you always know where you should go in the event of a fire.

You could meet here!

Hey, squirt! Look up, down, across, forward, backward, and diagonally for these words.

FIRE	STOP	HYDRANT	HOT
SAFETY	DROP	CANDLE	WATER
LOW	ROLL	TRUCK	CALL
GO	COOL	DRY	RESCUE

```
S T O P D W C E
A E R H R O A U
F L E R O L L C
E D T L P T L S
T N A R D Y H E
Y A W F I R E R
K C U R T D G O
```

Emergency Services

Emergency Services protect and serve your community. They are **first responders** to urgent and dangerous situations. Three primary emergency services can be summoned directly by the public:

Police are part of local, state, or federal law enforcement. Police help maintain public order and safety, enforce the law, and prevent, detect, and investigate criminal activities. These functions are known as **policing**.

Firefighters limit and extinguish the spread and threat of fire. Firefighters rescue people before turning their full attention to putting out the fire.

Emergency Medical Services (also known as **EMS**, **ambulance**, or **paramedic**) treat illnesses and injuries that require urgent medical care. EMS workers provide on-the-scene treatment, then transport to a medical facility.

Where is Spot?
He is ready to go
way up high.

Read and discuss this page with your parents.

There may be times when you are not near a trusted adult. Following some simple rules will help keep you safe.

Circle what you should do.

ALWAYS / NEVER talk to a stranger unless he/she is a safe adult.

ALWAYS / NEVER take anything from a stranger—even if he/she knows your name or has something of yours.

ALWAYS / NEVER go with a stranger or someone you don't trust.

ALWAYS / NEVER go near a stranger's car.

ALWAYS / NEVER let someone know where you are. Follow the rules about places you are permitted and not permitted to go.

ALWAYS / NEVER stay with a buddy or group of friends if you can. Help your friends make smart decisions. There is safety in numbers!

Safe Adults

Some people we don't know can be trusted to help. For example **Police Officers**, **Firefighters**, and **Paramedics** come to our aid, so we can think of them as **safe adults**.

Often, safe adults work in public places where they are doing their job— **teachers**, **bus drivers** and **store employees** for example.

You cannot tell if someone is safe just by the way he/she dresses, looks or talks. Just because a stranger knows your name, address, friend's or pet's name, or other personal things, doesn't make the person a safe adult.

Talk to your parents about who else you can trust and how to contact them. **Neighbors** and **relatives** are good people to know.

Write down names to remember.

_____

_____

_____

My Safety Information

When you have an emergency, call: **911**

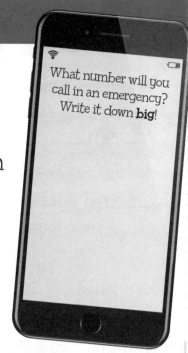

What number will you call in an emergency? Write it down **big**!

If you need to call **911**, tell the operator as many details as possible. Keep calm and tell them **where** you are, **what** is happening, **who** you are with, and **who** you are. Stay on the phone and answer the operator's questions.

Never call **911** unless you have a real emergency!

It is important to know your location and be able to tell the correct address and closest streets or landmarks.

What is your address? (Include 2 buildings or landmarks nearby.)

_____

_____

_____

_____

What is your telephone number?

_____

_____

Remember: NEVER call **911** unless you have a **real** emergency!

Is that an emergency?

Color the phones **red** in situations that are an emergency. Color them **blue** for non-emergency situations.

You scrape your knee.

Grandpa fell off a ladder, hit his head and is talking funny.

You get a bloody nose because it's a hot day.

Your friend was knocked off his bike and cannot wake up.

Mom fell down the stairs and broke her leg.

Grandma complains of chest pain.

You accidentally drank poison.

A friend gets a prickle in his foot.

There is a storm outside that is scary.

Your sister is bleeding from a cut.

Your mom grounds you and takes your toys away.

You and your aunt were in a car accident and she is trapped.

Your dad has a cold.

A friend stole your new toy and won't give it back.

No one else is home, and a man is peeking in your windows.

You cannot find your cat.

You think you saw a pink dinosaur wandering down the road.

The ice-cream man kept driving and didn't stop.

Smoke and fire is coming out of a neighbor's window.

The baby-sitter is choking and can't talk.

Community Helpers

There are many ways people help in our community.
Circle the **busy people** who have helped you.

A **hairdresser** cuts and
styles your hair.

A **veterinarian** helps
when your pet is sick.

A **mechanic** fixes cars
and trucks.

A **babysitter** looks after
kids when parents are out.

A **waiter** will bring
yummy food.

A **crossing guard** helps
you cross the street.

An **optometrist** makes
sure your eyes are healthy.

A **zoo-keeper** looks after
animals at the zoo.

A **doctor** helps keep
you healthy.

A **builder** constructs houses and offices.

A **chef** cooks food you love to eat.

A **farmer** grows the food you eat.

A **dentist** cleans and fixes your teeth.

WHAT WILL YOU BE?

A **teacher** helps you become smarter!

Draw yourself!

Tools of the Trade

Doctors help keep us healthy and take care of us when we are sick. Circle each of the doctor's tools.

Firefighters put out fires and help to rescue people. Circle each of the firefighter's tools.

Chefs cook our food when we go out to eat.
Circle each of the chef's tools.

Teachers work at a school and help children learn amazing stuff!
Circle each of the teacher's tools.

School Rules!

Schools are some of the most important places in a community. This is where children become educated in reading, writing, math, history, science, music, art, physical fitness, library skills, and much more.

There may be **home schools**, **preschools**, **elementary**, **middle**, and **high schools** for children. There may also be a **community college** for adults.

What is the **name** of your school?

_____

How do you **get** to school?

Bus   **Car**   **Walk**   **Bike**   Train

Who are some of your **Teachers**?

_____

_____

Name two places/buildings you pass by on your way to school.

_____

_____

Family, friends, and people from the community attend events at the **high school**. Perhaps they will see you! Circle any activity you would like to be part of.

 School play

 Sports team

 Speech

 Band

 Chorus

 Orchestra

 Art show

 Academic team

 Fashion show

 Fundraiser

Children learn more than reading, writing, and arithmetic at school. You will also learn how to be a good member of a community. This is called **good citizenship**.

Being a good citizen starts with **following the rules** you learn in school:

* Listen quietly to direction.
* Be kind and considerate.
* Wait your turn—don't cut in!
* Wash hands before eating.
* Wash hands after using the bathroom.
* Say please and thank you.
* Don't demand too much attention.
* Play fair—be a good sport.
* Treat others with respect.
* Help clean up.
* Return things you borrow.
* Share!

How can you be a good citizen at **home**?

How can you be a good citizen at **school**?

How can you be a good citizen in your **community**?

Shhhhhh...

Do you have a community **Library**? This is where anyone in your community can go to read, study, research, or borrow books and movies.

A **Librarian** can help you find information or select a good book to read.

People read and study in a library, so it is a quiet place. Always be respectful of others and talk in a whisper while you are at the library.

The library has sections for many kinds of books.

Draw a line from each book to the section in which it belongs on the shelf.

Fiction	**Nonfiction**	**Biography**	**Poetry**	**Reference**
Stories that are made up	Stories or accounts that are factual	Books about a real person	Books of verses and poetry	Information or instruction books

Splish-Splash!

Do you have a community **Pool**? This is where your friends and neighbors can relax, swim, and enjoy the sun. A **Lifeguard** is on duty to make sure everyone obeys the pool rules, and to rescue anyone having trouble in the water.

Rules help us stay safe and be respectful of others in our community. Always know your POOL RULES.

Wear a swim vest if you are a beginner swimmer. No jumping or diving unless from a diving board. Respect other people in the pool—no big splashing or dunking!

Use the code to find the message!

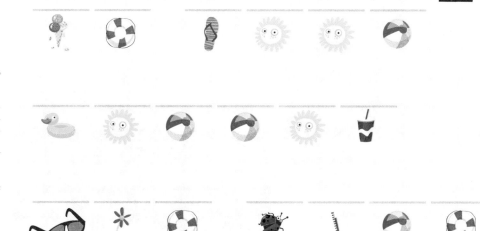

Answer: BE COOL—FOLLOW THE RULES!

From Seed to Sale

Do you have a community **Garden**? A community garden is a planting area where people can come and either help with the garden or have their own small plot. If Mary grows hundreds of tomatoes, she might share with Joe who grows beans and Liam who grows squash. A great way to spend a sunny day is to help plant, tend, or harvest fresh, natural veggies!

Veggies and fruit are good for you—the more colorful, the better! Color all these, and circle your favorites.

Do you have a community **Farmer's Market**? A farmer's market is where local **Farmers** bring fresh fruits and vegetables to sell. Some produce may come from the community garden. You can meet the people who grow the food! You might even be able to buy fresh milk from a local dairy, or honey from a beekeeper.

In the Cart

Do you have a local **Grocery Store**?
When you were little, did you ever sit in the grocery cart as it went up and down the aisles? There are so many foods to choose from. Apples! Cereal! Ice Cream! Cheese snacks!

You'll see many people from your community at the grocery store. Some are shopping for a big cookout. Some are shopping for family meals. Some are stocking up on food to put into the freezer. Everyone goes to the grocery store!

The grocery store is divided up into several sections. If you can't find an item, a **Store Clerk** can help you.

Look at each item and department code on this receipt. Write the item in the correct category section.

STEP-UP KIDS
A105 EarlyBird Lane
1-888-673-3266

****
RECEIPT
****

DESCRIPTION	DEP.	PRICE
apples	PR	$2.20
hot dogs	MT	$3.99
bag of peas	FZ	$1.87
bread	BK	$2.50
cake	BK	$12.99
carrots	PR	$3.99
cereal	DG	$4.80
donuts	BK	$0.99
eggs	DA	$1.20
bananas	PR	$0.80
ham	MT	$8.93
ice cream	FZ	$3.99
milk	DA	$2.69
chips	DG	$1.89
pizza	FZ	$2.69
soup	DG	$1.98
steak	MT	$6.70
yogurt	DA	$1.30

****

Total	$65.50
Cash	$70.00
Change	$4.50

****
Bank card   --- --- --- 6789
Approval Code   #123456
****

THANK YOU!

 PRODUCE

 BAKERY

 DAIRY

 FROZEN

 MEATS

 DRY GOODS

Dry goods include canned and boxed items.

Bow-Wow!

Do you have a community **Animal Shelter**? Dogs and cats at the shelter need homes with animal-loving humans. This is a special place where animals are brought that have no owners. Sometimes they are full-grown. Sometimes there are puppies and kittens at the shelter.

The animals may be treated by a **Veterinarian**, but most of the feeding, walking, and care is provided by **Volunteers**—regular people, just like you!

There are lots and lots of dogs or cats to choose from at the animal shelter. Look at all these! Every animal has an exact match—except for one doggy and one kitty. Can you find them?

Post Office

Do you have a local **Post Office**? The post office is where all the mail comes for your community. The mail is then sorted into bundles for each **Mail Carrier**. Your mail carrier brings your mail to your home and the homes near you. Some people have a box at the post office where their mail is placed each day.

If you have packages to mail, you can take them to the post office. The **Postal Worker** will weigh each one and let you know how much the postage (cost) will be. Then, off each package goes to be shipped, sorted, and delivered to the happy receiver!

It's fun to check the mail each day. There may be advertising pamphlets, bills to pay, or best of all, letters from friends and family—like a birthday card or an invitation to a party! If you like getting something in the mail, you can bet someone would love to get a letter from you. They might even write back!

Design the stamp!

Add someone's address. Don't forget the stamp!

From:

To:

What do I drive?

Match each helper with his or her vehicle.
Which helper doesn't have a match?

Signs are very important in a community. You have seen signs along the road while you ride in a car. Signs quickly give information to people about what is ahead, or what rule they should follow. There are also signs in your school and other buildings. There may be signs near the park or playground.

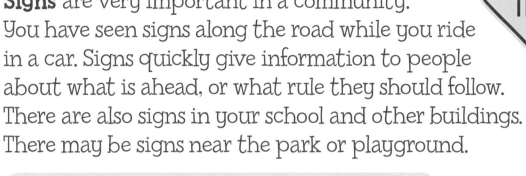

Each sign has a letter. Find the sign's meaning in the list and write in the sign's letter.

_____ Playground is near
_____ School crosswalk
_____ Don't cross the street yet
_____ This street goes one way
_____ Come to a complete stop
_____ Here is the door to leave
_____ A place to eat is ahead
_____ Don't litter!
_____ Stop and check for cars or bikes before you go on
_____ Buckle your seatbelt —it's the law!
_____ This is poisonous! Don't touch!
_____ You can now cross the street
_____ Railroad tracks are here
_____ This is the lane for bikes
_____ A hospital is up ahead

Money Money Money

Do you have a community **Bank**? Banks are very important in the community. Banks are where you can take your money to deposit. The bank keeps your money safe until you need it. This is good plan. After all, you don't want to keep all your money in a box under your bed.

Many banks have **Loan Officers**. A loan officer helps people borrow money to make a large purchase, like a new house.

A **Bank Teller** can help you deposit or withdraw your money. She can also cash a check for you that a relative sent for your birthday. Oh, boy! Cash!

Bank tellers count a lot of money all day. How good are you at **counting money**?

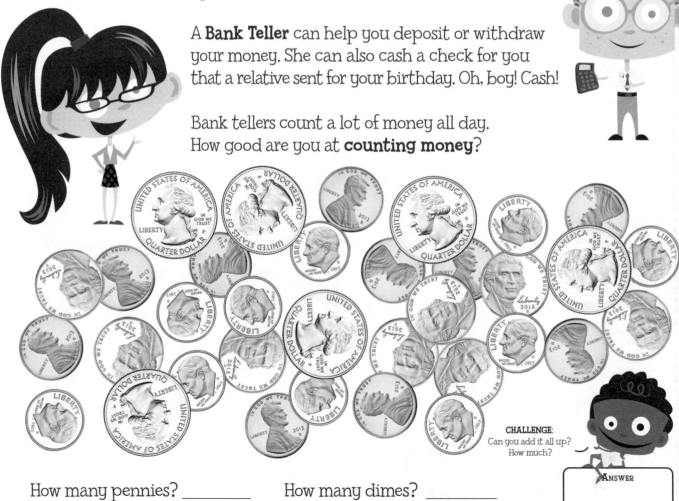

CHALLENGE:
Can you add it all up?
How much?

ANSWER

How many pennies? _____   How many dimes? _____

How many nickels? _____   How many quarters? _____

Tell about your community
—a unique place to live!

Write or draw about the **best places to...**

play

learn

shop

eat

visit

Neighborhood Scavenger Hunt

Take a walk around your neighborhood with an adult.
How many of these can you find?